weblinks

You don't need a computer to use this book. But, for readers who do have access to the Internet, the book provides links to recommended websites which offer additional information and resources on the subject.

You will find weblinks boxes like this on some pages of the book.

weblinks

For more information about Sugababes, go to www.waylinks.co.uk/ 21CentLives/PopGroups

waylinks.co.uk

To help you find the recommended websites easily and quickly, weblinks are provided on our own website, **waylinks.co.uk**. These take you straight to the relevant websites and save you typing in the Internet address yourself.

Internet safety

➚ Never give out personal details, which include: your name, address, school, telephone number, email address, password and mobile number.

➚ Do not respond to messages which make you feel uncomfortable – tell an adult.

➚ Do not arrange to meet in person someone you have met on the Internet.

➚ Never send your picture or anything else to an online friend without a parent's or teacher's permission.

➚ If you see anything that worries you, tell an adult.

A note to adults
Internet use by children should be supervised. We recommend that you install filtering software which blocks unsuitable material.

Website content

The weblinks for this book are checked and updated regularly. However, because of the nature of the Internet, the content of a website may change at any time, or a website may close down without notice. While the Publishers regret any inconvenience this may cause readers, they cannot be responsible for the content of any website other than their own.

21st CENTURY LIVES
POP GROUPS

Liz Gogerly

WAYLAND

First published in 2007 by Wayland

Reprinted in 2007 and 2008

Copyright © Wayland 2007

Editor: Hayley Fairhead
Design: Proof Books

Wayland
338 Euston Road
London NW1 3BH

Wayland
Level 17/207 Kent Street
Sydney, NSW 2000

Gogerly, Liz
   Pop groups. - (21st century lives)
   1. Rock groups - Juvenile literature 2. Rock musicians -
   Biography - Juvenile literature
   I. Title
   781.6'6'0922

ISBN 978-0-7502-5044-3

Printed in China

Wayland is a division of Hachette Children's Books,
an Hachette Livre UK company
www.hachettelivre.co.uk

Cover: Rap/hip-hop band the Black Eyed Peas pose for the camera.
Picture acknowledgements: Lisa O'Connor/Corbis: front cover and 8,
Tom Shaw/Getty Images for The Prince's Trust: title page and 17,
Dave Hogan/Getty Images: 4, Tim Mosenfelder/Getty Images: 5,
S.I.N/Corbis: 6, China Fotopress/Getty Images: 7, Fabrice
Cofferini/AFP/Getty Images; 9, Rune Hellestad/Corbis: 10, Shaun
Botterill/Getty Images: 11, Andrew Stuart/AFP/Getty Images: 12, Jeff J.
Mitchell/Getty Images: 13, Scott Wintrow/Getty Images: 14, Dave
Hogan/Getty Images: 15, 16, 18, 19, Vince Bucci/Getty Images: 20,
Ethan Miller/Getty Images: 21.

Contents

Arctic Monkeys
Top of the Tree

Arctic Monkeys collect the prize for Best Album at the Mercury Music Awards, 2006.

" Before the hysteria started, labels would say: 'I like you, but I'm not sure about this bit, and that song could do with changing...'. We never listened. And once it all kicked off we didn't even worry about it anymore. In London, the kids were watching the band and the record company were at the back watching the kids watching the band. "

Alex Turner
www.ilikemusic.com/features/
Arctic-Monkeys-Biography-1581

Band members:
Alex Turner (vocals and guitar)
Jamie 'Cookie' Cook (guitar)
Matt 'The Cat' Helders (drums)
Nick O'Malley (bass)

Date and place the band was formed:
2002, Sheffield

Sounds like: Snappy songs with loud guitars and crashing drums. Alex Turner's witty lyrics are about life on the street or the dancefloor, all sung in his distinct Northern accent.

Looks like: Four ordinary teenage lads queuing for the bus in town on a Saturday afternoon.

Top singles: *I Bet You Look Good on the Dancefloor* (Number 1 in UK, 2005), *When the Sun Goes Down* (Number 1 in UK, 2006), *Leave Before the Lights Come On* (2006).

Top albums: *Whatever People Say I Am, That's What I'm Not* (Number 1, 2006), *Favourite Worst Nightmare* (Number 1, 2007).

Awards and major achievements:
In 2006, the band scooped the Brit Award for Best British Breakthrough Act and the *NME* Award for Best New Band and Best British Band. Earlier that year they hit the record books when *Whatever People Say I Am, That's What I'm Not* became the fastest selling album of all time. The album also earned them the much-respected Mercury Prize and an Ivor Novella award in 2006. The band's two albums have won Best Album at the Brits in 2007 and 2008, and they were voted Best British Group in 2008.

Something you might not know about them: The Arctic Monkeys have not let fame go to their heads — lead singer Alex Turner still plays football for his pub football team.

In January 2006, the Arctic Monkeys stormed to the top of the album charts. *Whatever People Say I Am, That's What I'm Not* was the fastest-selling debut album ever. It seemed astonishing that a group of ordinary teenagers from Sheffield could cause such a stir. But so is the story so far…

Success has come quickly for the Arctic Monkeys. It all began in 2002 when boyhood chums Alex Turner and Jamie Cook asked for guitars for Christmas. Neither of them could play a note but they loved music. They listened to The Smiths, The Clash, Oasis (see page 22) and hip-hop bands like Roots Manuva. In his bedroom at home, Alex was writing lyrics of his own. Alex met the drummer Matthew Helders at college and the bassist Nicholson tagged on later. The Arctic Monkeys was born, yet the boys were barely 16 years old.

Arctic Monkeys have become known for their exciting live gigs.

In early 2003, the Arctic Monkeys started rehearsing in a warehouse in a run-down part of Sheffield called Neepseed. In June, they made their first live appearance at a pub in the centre of town. By word of mouth, the band became popular. At first they gave away demos of their songs to the crowd. Then they decided to make some of their songs available for download on the Internet. The buzz surrounding the band just got bigger as people began downloading their songs. Now the atmosphere at the gigs was electric. The crowd knew the words to the songs and joined in with the band. This was extraordinary and a first in British popular music – the band hadn't released a record but they had made a breakthrough using the Internet. By the end of 2004, the band was making the news. Radio and newspapers were interested in them, as were major record companies. The band turned down record deals because they didn't want to be told what to do.

In June 2005, the band eventually signed to Domino, a small record label run from the home of its owner Laurence Bell. By now, the Arctic Monkeys had thousands of fans eager to buy their records. In October, they had their first number one single, *I Bet You Look Good on the Dancefloor*. More number one singles, record-breaking album sales, success in America, as well as numerous industry awards have catapulted the Arctic Monkeys into stardom. But they continue to do things their own way. They shun the limelight and turn down many interviews and appearances. They like to keep things simple – perhaps that is the secret of their success.

"I like him [Alex Turner], I do, and he is definitely a bit of a genius lyricist, but he is still a kid. He was eight when *Definitely Maybe* came out."

Liam Gallagher of Oasis, Q Magazine

weblinks

For more information about the Arctic Monkeys, go to
www.waylinks.co.uk/21CentLives/PopGroups

Coldplay
Post-Britpop Giants

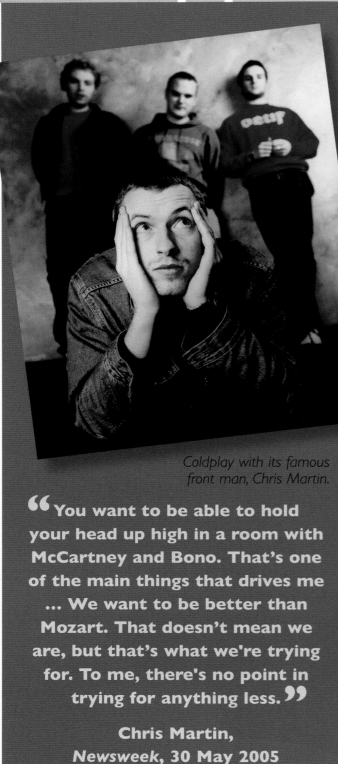

Coldplay with its famous front man, Chris Martin.

Band members:
Chris Martin (vocals, keyboard and guitar)
Jon Buckland (guitar)
Will Champion (drums)
Guy Berryman (bass guitar)

Date and place the band was formed: 1997, London

Sounds like: A combination of loud melodic guitars and keyboards with bursts of sweet, tortured lyrics. Coldplay is one of the most exciting alternative rock bands of its generation and produces some of the best love songs you're likely to hear.

Looks like: Most people recognize lead singer Chris Martin but they would struggle to remember the other three. With their casual clothes and normal haircuts, they don't stand out from the crowd.

Top singles: *Shiver* (2000), *Yellow* (2000), *Don't Panic* (2001), *Trouble* (2002), *In My Place* (2002), *The Scientist* (2003), *Clocks* (2003), *Speed of Sound* (2005), *Fix You* (2005), *The World Turned Upside Down* (2005), *Talk* (2006), *Violet Hill*, (2008), *Viva la Vida* (2008).

Top albums: *Parachutes* (Number 1, 2000), *A Rush of Blood to the Head* (Number 1, 2002), *X&Y* (Number 1, 2005), *Viva la Vida or Death and All His Friends* (Number 1, 2008).

Awards and major achievements: Since 2001, Coldplay have scooped six Brit Awards and four Grammy Awards.

Something you might not know about them: Singer Chris Martin became more interested in campaigning for fair trade after he travelled to Haiti with the relief agency Oxfam. During the band's tour of 2003/04 they collected over 4 million signatures for Oxfam's fair trade petition.

> "You want to be able to hold your head up high in a room with McCartney and Bono. That's one of the main things that drives me ... We want to be better than Mozart. That doesn't mean we are, but that's what we're trying for. To me, there's no point in trying for anything less."
>
> **Chris Martin,**
> *Newsweek, 30 May 2005*

Martin at the keyboards: Coldplay has bought the piano back to the forefront of modern music.

Coldplay is one of the most successful British bands of the past decade. The group plays sell-out gigs in America and its third album, *X&Y*, went to number one in 28 countries.

As rock bands go, Coldplay has a squeaky clean image. Singer Chris Martin is the son of an accountant and teacher. He looks after himself by doing yoga and he doesn't drink or smoke. Martin met the rest of the band at University College in London, in 1996. By 1998, Coldplay was spending time away from their studies to play live gigs in London. In 1999, they released their first record single, *Brothers and Sisters*. A record deal with Parlophone was signed later that year and in 2000 they released their debut album, *Parachutes*.

One of the most played songs of summer 2000 was Coldplay's *Yellow*. The single went to number four in the UK charts and when the band played at Glastonbury festival the crowd sang along. In July 2000, the album *Parachutes* reached number one. Coldplay had cracked it in the UK. The world tour of 2002 helped to establish them as one of the top international acts, packing stadiums and sport arenas everywhere they went.

In September 2002, Coldplay's second album, *A Rush of Blood to the Head*, went to number one in the UK and Canada. It went on to become the tenth biggest selling album of the year in America. Around the same time, Chris Martin married Hollywood actress Gwyneth Paltrow.

Fans waited eagerly for the third Coldplay album: *X&Y* is a daring album with larger than life songs. Once again, Coldplay had produced a winner and *X&Y* went on to become the best selling album of 2005. Coldplay returned to the studio soon after in 2006, but it wasn't until 2008 that they released *Viva la Vida or Death and All His Friends*. It went on to be number one in 36 countries and became the most paid-for downloaded album of all time.

"Confident, bold, ambitious, bunged with singles and impossible to contain, *X&Y* doesn't reinvent the wheel but it does reinforce Coldplay as the band of their time… This is a great, great record that has just raised the bar for everyone."

Paul McNamee, *NME*

weblinks

For more information about Coldplay, go to
www.waylinks.co.uk/21CentLives/PopGroups

Black Eyed Peas
Pop Meets Hip-Hop

The Black Eyed Peas can always strike a pose for the camera.

Band members:
William Adams – will.i.am
Allen Pineda – apl.de.ap
Jamie Gomez – Taboo
Stacy Ferguson – Fergie

Date and place the band was formed: 1998, Los Angeles, California, USA

Sounds like: Black Eyed Peas (BEP) bridge the gap between many sounds and influences. They are often described as a rap/hip-hop band but they aren't scared to experiment with different styles such as funk, Latin rhythms or even Filipino folk rock! Expect to hear all kinds of instruments too. Listen out for kazoos and tubas as well as 40-piece orchestras!

Looks like: Exciting, vibrant and unpredictable.

Top singles: *Where is the Love?* (Number 1, 2003), *Hey Mama* (2004), *Let's Get It Started* (2004), *Don't Phunk with My Heart* (2005), *Don't Lie* (2005), *My Humps* (2005), *Pump It* (2006).

Top albums: *Bridging the Gap* (2000), *Elephunk* (2003), *Monkey Business* (2005).

Awards and major achievements: Two Grammy Awards, including the award for Best Rap Performance for *Don't Phunk With My Heart,* in 2006.

Something you might not know about them: Will-i-am helped to co-found the Peapod Foundation, a charity which helps disadvantaged children all around the world. In May 2006, BEP organized a benefit gig in South Africa for the charity.

> 66 **We like human error. Nothing should ever be perfect. If our drummer messes up and comes out of it, it's like: 'Dang, dog! You did it!'. It makes every show, every night, different, because of the spontaneity and the ability to stop it, slow it down, bring the energy up or bring the energy lower.** 99
>
> **will.i.am**
> **Interview with *Vh1*, August 2003**

The Black Eyed Peas create a unique sound, they deliver rap with a positive message, and they perform some of the most exciting live gigs in the world today.

The band started when high school friends will.i.am (William Adams) and apl.de.ap (Allen Pineda) began break-dancing and rapping together at clubs in Los Angeles, California. In the late 1980s and early 1990s, the stars of hip-hop had a hard gangsta style and the lyrics were about street issues. Will.i.am and apl.de.ap looked the part but their songs had a more peaceful message. The band soon signed to the hip-hop label Ruthless Records. They named the group Atban Klann, recruited more band members and recorded the album *Grass Roots*.

Grass Roots was never released because the record label didn't think it would do well. The band was disappointed but it gave them the kick they needed. In 1995, will.i.am and apl.de.ap changed the name of the group to Black Eyed Peas (BEP). Taboo (Jamie Gomez) joined the band and they ploughed on with live performances. In 1998, BEP released their debut album *Behind the Front*. Next came the 2000 album, *Bridging the Gap*. Neither album did particularly well. It took a new singer, Stacy 'Fergie' Ferguson, and a stunning third album to change their fortune.

Elephunk was released in 2003. The anti-war song *Where is the Love?* was written after the terrorist attack on the Twin Towers in New York. It tapped into the feeling of many people at that time and stayed at number one in the UK charts for six weeks. Suddenly BEP was big news. In 2005, they released their album *Monkey Business*. Once again, the band took risks with their musical styles. Some people criticised the band for their lyrics (some didn't like the sexual suggestiveness of songs like *My Humps*, while others

*Lights, camera, action, action, action...
BEP are a thrilling act.*

didn't think they were tough enough) and hip-hop fans felt they had sold out. However, the album topped the charts, and singles such as *Don't Phunk with My Heart* and *My Humps* were huge hits. No matter what people think about BEP they have brought rap and hip-hop music to a whole new audience.

"Black Eyed Peas have clearly found a magic formula for success: good-guy rap plus pop-profundity multiplied by numerous special guests."

Betty Clark
The *Guardian*, May 2005

weblinks

For more information about
Black Eyed Peas, go to
www.waylinks.co.uk/21CentLives/PopGroups

Sugababes
Girls at the Top

Sugababes: sweet, sexy and sassy.

66 We don't focus on trying to be different from other girl bands, we just experiment with different sounds and write about what we know. I think people pick up on the fact that we are being ourselves and keeping it real. **99**

Heidi Range
http://www.girl.com.au/
sugababesinterview.htm

Band members:
Keisha Buchanan
Heidi Range
Amelle Berrabah

Date and place the band was formed: 1999, London

Sounds like: Perfect pop music with a twist. The basis of the Sugababes' sound is the three-part, all-girl vocals. Mix in R'n'B, hip-hop and garage influences and you have the street-wise sound that is distinctly Sugababes.

Looks like: Three fashionable friends dressed for a night out clubbing. Hair, make-up and clothes all look cool.

Top singles: *Overload* (2000), *Freak Like Me* (Number 1, 2002), *Round and Round* (Number 1, 2002), *Hole in The Head* (Number 1, 2003), *Push the Button* (Number 1, 2005), *Ugly* (2005), *Red Dress* (2006), *About You Now* (Number 1, 2007).

Top albums: *One Touch* (2000), *Angels with Dirty Faces* (2002), *Three* (2003), *Taller in More Ways* (Number 1, 2005), *Overloaded: The Singles Çollection* (2006), *Change* (Number 1, 2007).

Awards and major achievements:
A Brit Award for Best British Dance Act in 2003. When the album *Taller in More Ways* went to number one in 2005, Sugababes was number one in the singles, airplay and download charts at the same time.

Something you might not know about them: The girls co-write many of their songs. Usually, each girl comes up with one verse and they all come together to make the chorus.

Amelle, Keisha and Heidi have a refreshing and distinct three-part vocal.

The Sugababes has gone through two major shake-ups but they have still chalked up five number one singles. No other modern female band has made six hit albums and managed to keep on top of the business for so long.

Mutya Buena and Keisha Buchanan were childhood friends. They sang together and dreamed about making it as pop stars. They met Siobhan Donaghy at a party and decided to form the band. Mutya and Keisha were just 14 when they were signed to London Records. A year later, their debut single, *Overload*, went to number six in the charts and the band was nominated for a Brit Award. In 2001, the record label dropped the girls and Siobhan left shortly afterwards. Heidi Range, who used to sing with rival girl band Atomic Kitten, stepped into her shoes.

The group was signed to Island Records. In the studio the girls experimented with new sounds. *Freak Like Me* is driven by samples taken from Gary Numan's 1979 hit *Are Friends Electric?* The song went to the top of the singles chart in 2002 and brought the Sugababes the fame they had long dreamed about. The next single, *Round Round*, went to number one and the second album, *Angels With Dirty Faces*, reached number six in the album charts. The hits kept coming. In 2005, the Sugababes reached number one in the single and album charts with *Push the Button* and the album *Taller in More Ways*.

Founder member Mutya left the Sugababes in December 2005 to start a solo career. Many people didn't think the band could survive another change but new singer Amelle Berrabah fitted in well. With further hit singles, a chart-topping album *Changes* and a country-wide tour in 2007, the Sugababes keep going from strength to strength. Their sixth album, due to be released at the end of 2008, is bound to be a success.

weblinks

For more information about Sugababes, go to
www.waylinks.co.uk/21CentLives/PopGroups

"The Sugababes have broken almost every rule in the pop book. When they were dropped in 2001 they came back, better than before, with a number one. They are sexy without having ever sold themselves on sex; they're outspoken and gutsy, but their peers admire them rather than fear their ability to steal their boyfriends. Teens love them, but so do their parents."

Peter Robinson
The *Observer*, 18 September 2005

Kaiser Chiefs
English Eccentrics

Kaiser Chiefs step out on the red carpet.

Band members:
Ricky Wilson (vocals, tambourine)
Andrew 'Whitey' White (guitar)
Simon Rix (bass guitar)
Nick 'Peanut' Baines (drums)
Nick Hodgson (keyboards)

Date and place the band was formed: 2003, Leeds

Sounds like: An indie guitar band which harks back to the sound of new wave British bands such as The Jam, Madness and The Specials, and Brit-pop giants Blur.

Looks like: English eccentrics with messy hair, a touch of make-up, charity shop suits, natty ties and pork pie hats.

Top singles: *I Predict a Riot* (2004 and 2005), *Oh My God* (2004 and 2005), *Everyday I Love You Less and Less* (2005), *Modern Way* (2005), *Ruby* (Number 1, 2007), *Everything Is Average Nowadays* (2007).

Top albums: *Employment* (2005), *Yours Truly, Angry Mob* (2007), *Off With Their Heads* (2008).

Awards and major achievements: The band was stunned when they picked up Brit awards for Best British Group, Best British Rock Act and Best British Live Act at the 2006 Brit Awards. In 2006, they won *NME* awards for Best Album and singer Ricky Wilson won an award for Best Dressed.

Something you might not know about them: The band support Leeds United FC. They named themselves after the South African football club Kaizer Chiefs, for which Leeds captain Lucas Radebe once played.

> **We can be playing in front of 50,000 people in an arena and I'm thinking about Peanut wearing a scarf, rather than how amazing our journey as a band has been. Instead of getting awestruck, you get a new level of reality. We are still the same normal five boys from Leeds.**

Ricky Wilson, The *Independent*, 17 August 2006

Singer Ricky Wilson found himself in plaster after one of his stage-diving episodes went wrong.

In the summer of 2003, five musical friends finally got their act together. They called themselves Kaiser Chiefs and played at the Leeds Festival. They were near the bottom of the bill. Just two years later Kaiser Chiefs was the opening act for the Live-8 concert in Philadelphia, USA. The world was at their fingertips.

Kaiser Chiefs is made up of school friends Simon, Nick (Peanut) Baines and Nick Hodgson. By the time they were 15, the boys were gigging around their hometown of Leeds. They named themselves Parva and played indie guitar or garage rock music. At the time, singer Ricky Wilson was with a Rolling Stones tribute band. His on-stage antics, dancing and jumping attracted Parva and they asked him to join their band.

Ricky Wilson joined up but Parva still didn't seem to be going anywhere. During the summer of 2003, they changed their name to Kaiser Chiefs and sharpened up their sound. They wrote about everyday life in Northern England. The formula worked and the band cracked the local gig circuit.

In 2004, Kaiser Chiefs self-financed their debut single, *Oh My God* and it got to number 66 in the charts. A record deal with B-Unique, an indie record label, followed. Their second single, *I Predict A Riot*, got to number 22 in the UK singles chart. The same year Kaiser Chiefs opened the *NME* Awards Show. Suddenly, the band was in demand.

Kaiser Chiefs re-released their first two singles in 2005. Both records stormed into the top ten. The debut album *Employment* got to number two in the UK, selling over 1 million copies. In 2006, the Kaiser Chiefs bounded up onto the stage at the Brits to accept three awards. Their second album is every bit as good as their first: one of the songs is called *Everything is Average These Days* – something you could never say of Kaiser Chiefs.

weblinks

For more information about the Kaiser Chiefs, go to
www.waylinks.co.uk/21CentLives/PopGroups

"Most importantly, it is giddy with good tunes. Every song here is hummable after one listen and wedged in the brain after two. That *Employment* is derivative is both undeniable and irrelevant. It is so confident, so smart, so full of life, that a more enjoyable 45 minutes is hard to imagine."

Dorian Lynsky reviews the album *Employment*, The *Guardian*, March 2005.

Gorillaz
Virtually Alive and Kicking

Band leader, Murdoc (right) and singer, 2D (left) of Gorillaz.

Band members:
2D (Stu-Pot) (vocals, keyboards)
Noodle (lead guitar, backing vocals)
Russel Hobbs (drums)
Murdoc Niccals (bass guitar)

Date and place the band was formed: 1998, London

Sounds like: Experimental – a mish mash of musical styles, combining pop, hip-hop, dub, rock and Latin. Listen out for the children's choir too.

Looks like: Gorillaz is the first 'virtual hip-hop group' so don't expect to see real human faces. Illustrator Jamie Hewlett has created a crew of colourful cartoon characters that look anarchic and totally twenty-first century.

Top singles: *Clint Eastwood (2001), Rock the House (2001), 911 (2001), Tomorrow Comes Today (2002), Feel Good Inc. (2005), Dare (Number 1, 2005), Dirty Harry (2005), Kids With Guns (2006).*

Top albums: *Gorillaz (2001), Demon Days* (Number 1, 2005).

Awards and major achievements: Gorillaz won a Grammy Award in 2005 for Best Pop Collaboration with Vocals. Gorillaz is in the *Guinness World Records* as the Most Successful Virtual Band.

Something you might not know about them: Illustrator Jamie Hewlett was one of the creators of the comic book *Tank Girl*.

> **"One day, we were home watching MTV with our eyes just kind of glazed. Because if you watch MTV for too long, it's a bit like hell – there's nothing of substance there. So we got this idea for a cartoon band, something that would be a comment on that."**

Jamie Hewlett talking about why he formed Gorillaz with singer Damon Albarn.

GORILLAZ

Gorillaz live events are a larger than life experience with images of the band projected onto huge screens.

At the 2006 Grammy Awards, Gorillaz fans were delighted when they saw their favourite virtual band take to the stage. Band members Murdoc Niccals, 2D, Russel Hobbs and Noodle looked larger than life. Clever visual effects made it appear that the four members of the group were actually performing with Madonna. It was an extraordinary moment, but everything about Gorillaz is extraordinary.

The cartoon band Gorillaz is the brainchild of Blur lead singer Damon Albarn and artist Jamie Hewlett. Hewlett drew the band members and, together with Albarn, made up a fictional life for the band. The story of the band was posted on the Internet. Fans could visit the official website and check out the band's studio and home. It was exciting and enticing for young fans surfing the web.

Gorillaz released the single *Tomorrow Comes Today* in 2000. By word of mouth the band grew in popularity. In March 2001, they released the first single *Clint Eastwood*. Its catchy chorus and lazy hip-hop style made it one of the smash hits of the year. The debut album *Gorillaz* went on to sell over 3 million copies in the UK and went platinum in the US. Amazingly, the band also went on tour. Fans could watch the cartoon group on a large screen. Meanwhile they could see the silhouettes of the 'real' group as they performed behind another screen.

In 2005, Gorillaz was back with the hit album *Demon Days*. Hewlett aged his cartoon characters and gave them a harder look. The sound was even more experimental. They were joined by guest performers like De La Soul, Blondie vocalist Debbie Harry and actor Dennis Hopper. Hit singles included the number one *DARE*, and *Feel Good Inc.*, which went to number two in the UK charts, and *Dirty Harry*, which featured the Children's Choir San Fernandez. The album *Demon Days* went to number one in the UK charts.

Band member Noodle has been 'killed off' (if a cartoon character can be done away with!) in the band's video for *El Mañana*. There are hints that the band may be quitting. However, with the Gorillaz appearance in the pop-opera *Monkey: Journey to the West* and Jamie Hewlett designing the opening sequence for the BBC's coverage of the Beijing Olympics in 2008, we may not have heard the last of the Gorrilaz.

"Before you even consider the sonic and melodic innovation paraded through the album there's so much crammed into each of these 15 songs (without any one of them sounding overproduced or cluttered) that repeated listening is a must."

Peter Robinson of *NME* reviews the album *Demon Days*.

weblinks

For more information about Gorillaz, go to
www.waylinks.co.uk/21CentLives/PopGroups

McFly
Boy band with Attitude

Cheeky chaps: McFly smile and play up for the fans.

Band members:
Danny Jones (lead guitar, vocals)
Dougie Poynter (bass guitar, vocals)
Tom Fletcher (rhythm guitar, piano, vocals)
Harry Judd (drums)

Date and place the band was formed:
2004, London

Sounds like: 1960s meets 1970s with injections of punk, pop and psychedelic sounds.

Looks like: Nice boys with hot haircuts and cool clothes.

Top singles: *Five Colours in Her Hair* (Number 1, 2004), *Obviously* (Number 1, 2004), *All About You/You've Got a Friend* (Number 1, 2005), *I'll be OK* (Number 1, 2005), *Please, Please/Don't Stop Me Now* (Number 1, 2006), *Baby's Coming Back/ Transylvania* (Number 1, 2007), *One for the Radio* (2008).

Top albums: *Room on the Third Floor* (Number 1, 2004), *Wonderland* (Number 1, 2005), *Motion in the Ocean* (2006), *Radio:ACTIVE* (2008).

Awards and major achievements: 2005 was a good year for McFly: they won the Brit Award for Best Pop Act and Smash Hit Awards for Stars of the Year, Best UK Band, Best Single, Best Album, Most Snoggable [sic] Male (Danny) and Top Mop (Dougie).

Something you might not know about them: In 2004, the band made an appearance in the BBC medical drama *Casualty*. The boys play themselves in the story about an injured McFly fan.

> **"The term boy band is kind of offensive – you think of Westlife and suits."** (Dougie)
> **"It's a weird phrase ... because to us, we're no less musicians than any other rock band out there. We work as hard, on the parts and the instruments."** (Tom)
>
> **Members of McFly describe how they feel about being described as a 'boy band'.**
> **The *Guardian*, 18 November 2005**

In the summer of 2006, McFly was back at the top of the singles chart. The cover of the Queen song *Don't Stop Me Now* was the boys' fifth number one hit and they celebrated in style. They stripped off and performed naked at a club in London.

The McFly story goes all the way back to 2001. Tom Fletcher auditioned for the band Busted. He lost out but made a deal with Busted's label instead. Later, Tom teamed up with guitarist Danny Jones. They called themselves McFly after the character Marty McFly from the 1980s sci-fi film *Back to the Future*. The boys advertised for other band members in the music magazine *NME*. Harry Judd and 15-year-old Dougie Poynter got the jobs.

At recent gigs McFly has covered classic tunes from the 1960s.

McFly may well be fresh-faced but they grew up listening to 1960s music by the Beatles and The Beach Boys. McFly brandish their musical influences with pride. The chart-topping debut single *Five Colours in Her Hair* has shades of punk with its tinny guitar riffs. They regularly cover The Who's *Pinball Wizard* at their concerts.

McFly's debut hit single was followed by *Obviously*, which also shot to the top of the charts. The album *Room on the Third Floor* soared to number one in the album charts. Suddenly, McFly was everywhere. Their pictures were plastered on girls' bedroom walls up and down the country and they were filling arenas. "I don't want to see lighters," Tom told the audience at Birmingham NEC. "I want to see your mobile phones in the air! We're taking the concert into the twenty-first century!"

In 2005, McFly released their second album, *Wonderland*. Many journalists who had slated MyFly in the past were pleasantly surprised. The band had matured and they sounded even better. The album topped the charts and there were two more number one singles. Proceeds from *All About You/You've Got a Friend* went to Comic Relief. In summer 2006, McFly starred in the teen movie *Just My Luck* and are continuing to rack up the hits. Now people are saying that it's talent, as well as luck, that has brought McFly so far, so quickly.

"McFly have got the lot: the hurtling around, the sweat, the bloody-minded determination — and the musical ability… They aren't the best-looking boys in school, they're the other ones, the inbetweeners who learned to get the girls by being funny."

Sophie Heawood, The *Guardian*,
17 September 2005

weblinks

For more information about McFly, go to
www.waylinks.co.uk/21CentLives/PopGroups

Girls Aloud
As Voted for by the People...

Girls Aloud: girls-next-door meet glitzy glamour.

Band members:
Cheryl Cole
Nadine Coyle
Sarah Harding
Nicola Roberts
Kimberley Walsh

Date and place the band was formed: 2002, London, on the *PopStars: The Rivals* TV talent show.

Sounds like: Fun, thoroughly girly pop music with a 1960s flavour and a rocking beat. All the girls can sing well and belt out the high notes for the ballads.

Looks like: Beautiful and sexy. High heels are a must!

Top singles: *Sound of the Underground* (Number 1, 2002), *No Good Advice* (2003), *Life Got Cold* (2003), *Jump* (2003), *The Show* (2004), *Love Machine* (2004), *I'll Stand By You* (Number 1, 2004), *Wake Me Up* (2005), *Long Hot Summer* (2005), *Biology* (2005), *See the Day* (2005), *Whole Lotta History* (2006), *Something Kinda Ooooh* (2006), *I Think We're Alone Now* (2006), *Sexy! No No No...* (2007), *Call the Shots* (2007), *Can't Speak French* (2007).

Top albums: *Sound of the Underground* (2003), *What Will the Neighbours Say* (2004), *Chemistry* (2005), *The Sound of Girls Aloud* (2006), *Tangled Up* (2007).

Awards and major achievements: Girls Aloud has beaten the Spice Girls' record of being the girl band with the most hit singles in a row: Girls Aloud has 15 hits to the Spice Girls' ten.

Something you might not know about them: On their 2006 tour, the girls did a cover of the Kaiser Chief's *I Predict a Riot*.

> **"I remember reading one of the gossip magazines in the early days. We'd been number one for three weeks and they said that was the only hit we were going to have. I cried after reading that because I didn't want it to end... I wish I could remember who wrote it because I would love to send them our THIRD album."**
>
> **Cheryl Cole,
> Girls Aloud official website.**

Two number one singles and three hit albums prove there is more to the girls than pretty faces.

When Girls Aloud's single, *Sound of the Underground*, went to number one at Christmas 2002 journalists thought they would be a one-hit wonder. By 2006, with 12 UK top ten hit singles and three UK top ten albums to their name, the girls had become queens of the quick hit.

Girls Aloud got to the top in an unusual way. They joined thousands of other young people in auditions for the TV talent show *Popstars: The Rivals*. Eventually, the viewing public voted for their favourite girls to be in the band. Girls Aloud was awarded a five-album record deal and management by Louis Walsh, the creator of Westlife. It was a recipe for success but many people didn't think a manufactured band would have the staying power to make it big.

The public vote went to Nadine Coyle, Cheryl Tweedy (now Cole), Nicola Roberts, Kimberley Walsh and Sarah Harding. Nadine is from Derry in Ireland but all the other girls come from the North of England. There is something girl-next-door about them, albeit they are very pretty. In 2006, Cheryl hit the headlines when she married England footballer Ashley Cole. Until then, the girls shared an apartment in London. In many ways success and fame hasn't changed them, which is part of their appeal.

In 2006, 2007 and 2008, Girls Aloud toured the UK. Now they play packed arenas. The shows are colourful and exciting with multiple costume changes and songs from musicals and covers of other bands. The girls have a bulging back catalogue of hit records, some of which they wrote themselves. Journalists who were quick to criticise the band when they first started give them good reviews. It seems like Girls Aloud are here for keeps!

'Girls Aloud aren't about polish and perfection. They're about fun, and they deliver it in heaps'

The *Telegraph*, May 2006

weblinks

For more information about Girls Aloud, go to
www.waylinks.co.uk/21CentLives/PopGroups

Green Day
American Superstars

The musical trio Green Day accept a Creative Voices Award in 2006.

Band members:
Billie Joe Armstrong (vocals, lead guitar)
Mike Dirnt (bass guitar)
Tré Cool (drums)

Date and place the band was formed: 1989, East Bay, California, USA

Sounds like: A blast from the past – all the energy of punk rock music with edge, attitude and a smattering of pop.

Looks like: Back in black. Since the release of *American Idiot* all the band wear black with a splash of red. Eyeliner and messed up hair complete the look.

Top singles: *Basket Case* (1995), *Geek Stink Breath* (1995), *Good Riddance/Time of Your Life* (1998), *Minority* (2000), *American Idiot* (2004), *Boulevard of Broken Dreams* (2004), *Holiday* (2005), *Wake Me Up When September Ends* (2005) *Jesus of Suburbia* (2005), *The Saints Are Coming* (2006), *Working Class Hero* (2007), *The Simpsons Themetune* (2007)

Top albums: *Dookie* (1994), *Insomniac* (1995), *Nimrod* (1997), *Warning* (2000), *American Idiot* (2004).

Awards and major achievements: Three Grammy Awards, most notably the 2005 Grammy for Best Rock Album (*American Idiot*). In 2006, they also won two Brit Awards for Best International Group and International Album (*American Idiot*).

Something you might not know about them: Look out for *American Idiot: The Motion Picture*. The film of the album *American Idiot* was shot in 2006. The band doesn't play a major role in the film but they make an appearance.

“I never get sick of playing it. I never get tired of hearing it. It always feels brand new. It always makes me feel emotional inside, and with that song, we can say that we've done something that no one else has done in rock music, and that is make this nine-minute anthem that's considered punk rock.”

Billie Joe Armstrong talking about the song *Jesus of Suburbia*, Spin, October 2005.

Green Day has always been about loud thrashing guitars. The American trio has been credited with reviving punk for a new generation. But, the release of *American Idiot* in 2004 has brought them superstar status. Now it's their politics as well as punk that's getting them noticed.

In the late 1980s, Billie Joe Armstrong and Mike Dirnt were just two Californian kids with a love of garage rock, sporting ripped jeans and t-shirts. All that changed when they picked up guitars and formed the band Sweet Children. However, a change of name and a deal with punk label Lookout! Records really set things in motion. The debut album *1,039/Smoothed Out Slappy Hours* was an underground success. At gigs, fans pogoed to the tunes and didn't care much that all Green Day sang about was bodily functions, cars and girls. In 1991, Tré Cool joined them on drums. The next album *Kerplunk!* was a success with a new generation of punk fans and the band began touring overseas.

Green Day signed to Reprise Records in 1994. The third album, *Dookie*, became their first commercial success. It also won them a Grammy for Best Alternative Album. The year 1994 was also memorable for Green Day's appearance at Woodstock 1994 (a rock festival to commemorate the anniversary of the hippie music festival Woodstock of 1969). The band began a giant mud fight with the audience and Dirnt had his front teeth punched out by a security guard. In 1997, with the release of *Nimrod* it was apparent that the band was making a change in direction. Armstrong's acoustic guitar on the single *Good Riddance (Time of Your Life)* heralded a new sound. There was also more depth to the lyrics.

After a few years break from the music scene Green Day bounced back in 2000 with the poppy album *Warning*. But, it was the release of *American Idiot* in 2004 that catapulted Green Day right back to the top of the game. They were having a go at American politics and President George Bush. The fans loved it and the album has sold more than six million copies worldwide. The Grammys and Brit Awards rolled in. Green Day had conquered the world.

Now Green Day use their fame to promote good causes. They recorded *The Saints Are Coming* with U2 for the victims of Hurricane Katrina in 2006 and *Working Class Hero* for Amnesty International's efforts for the human rights crisis in Darfur, Sudan.

The band's 2007 album brings a new chapter in Green Day's story.

"Green Day encore with an utterly sincere cover of Queen's *We Are The Champions*. The entire crowd sings along. It feels like Green Day are not just celebrating their return to the top of the charts; they're leading a rock and roll resistance movement."

Matt Hendrikson, reviewing Green Day's live gig at Brixton Academy, London, January 2005, *Rolling Stone* magazine.

weblinks

For more information about Green Day, go to
www.waylinks.co.uk/21CentLives/PopGroups

Other Pop Groups

Oasis

In 1994, Manchester band Oasis soared to the top of the album charts with their first album, *Definitely Maybe*. At the time, it was the fastest selling debut album in the UK. Fronted by singer/songwriter and lead guitarist Noel Gallagher and his brother, singer/songwriter Liam Gallagher, Oasis has gone on to become a top-selling international band. They scored their first number one single with *Some Might Say* in 1995. Later that year came their huge hit album *(What's the Story) Morning Glory?*. It became the second best selling album of all-time in Britain. The third album, *Be Here Now*, became the fastest selling album in chart history. At the height of their fame, the Gallagher brothers were rarely out of the tabloids. Bad boy antics and outbursts against other bands often made the headlines. In 2005, Oasis were back in the news. The sixth album, *Don't Believe the Truth*, and the singles *Lyla* and *The Importance of Being Idle* all reached number one. In 2006, the band was voted Best Act in the World Today at the Q Awards and in 2008 the band started touring again to promote their seventh album *Dig Out Your Soul*.

The Kooks

The Kooks was formed in Brighton, in 2004. Members Luke Pritchard, Hugh Harris, Max Rafferty and Paul Garred are passionate about their record collections, which include vintage British bands such as The Police, The Kinks and The Smiths. They are also fans of Lou Reed, Jack Johnson and David Bowie (the group are named after a song on Bowie's classic album *Hunky Dory*). The influence of their favourite acts is unmistakeable but the band has a refreshing new sound that is natural and in sync with the new crop of guitar bands. Their debut album of 2006, *Inside In/Inside Out*, went to number two in the album charts. Singles *Naïve* and *She Moves in Her Own Way* have been top ten hits. Their follow-up album *Konk* reached number one in 2008 and, being festival favourites, this band is going to be around for a while yet.

Pussycat Dolls

The American R'n'B/hip-hop band Pussycat Dolls started out as a dance troupe. At their early performances at clubs in Los Angeles they covered 1960s classic hits. With their sexy outfits and vintage costumes they caused quite a sensation. The line-up was ever changing and even included guest appearances by Gwen Stefani, Christina Aguilera and Kelly Osbourne. Then, in 2003, the troupe appeared in the blockbuster movie *Charlie's Angels: Full Throttle*. The same year, Nicole Scherzinger, a winner of the TV show *American Popstars*, became the lead singer. In 2005, the girls released their first album *PCD*. Singles *Don't Cha* and *Stickwitu* were number one hits in the UK. *Beep* and *Buttons* also made the top ten. In 2006, Pussycat Dolls went on tour supporting the Black Eyed Peas (see page 8–9) and in 2008 released their second album *Doll Domination*.

Keane

Schoolfriends Tim Rice-Oxley, Tom Chaplin and Richard Hughes formed Keane in 1997 in Battle, East Sussex. Originally, they performed covers of their favourite bands: the Beatles, U2 and Oasis. However, Tim and Tom had been writing songs for years and decided to perform their own material at some of their London pub gigs. In 2002, the band released its first single, *Everybody's Changing*, through the indie label Fierce Panda Records. The band caused a stir because it didn't use guitars. It was the first piano rock band for decades. A major deal with Island Records and the number three single, *Somewhere Only We Know*, followed. The debut album *Hopes and Fears* went to number one, becoming the second bestselling album of 2004 in the UK. In 2005, the band won the Brit

Awards for Best Album and Best Breakthrough Band, as voted by listeners of BBC Radio 1. They topped the album charts again in 2006 with their second album *Under the Iron Sea* and big things and a different sound are expected for their third album, *Perfect Symmetry*, due out at the end of 2008.

Franz Ferdinand

Scottish band Franz Ferdinand was formed in 2001. The post-punk, art-rock band has two hit albums, *Franz Ferdinand* (2004) and *You Could Have it So Much Better* (2005). The band was started by singer Alex Kapranos and bassist Robert Hardy in Glasgow. Nicholas McCarthy (lead guitar) and Paul Thomson (drums) joined them soon after and they started playing gigs in empty warehouses or buildings in the city. They soon got a reputation for staging exciting events, which were a platform for music and art. The Domino record label offered them a deal in 2003 and they released their self-titled debut album in early 2004. The album reached number three in the UK and was a minor hit in the US. It also earned them the 2004 Mercury Music Prize and they won the 2005 Brit Awards for Best Group and Best Rock Act, as voted for by readers of *Kerrang*. The band finally made it big in America in 2005. The album *You Could Have it So Much Better* was a top ten hit in the US and reached number one in the UK.

U2

Irish rock band U2 is one of the most enduring and popular bands in the world today. The band was formed in 1976 by drummer Larry Mullen. He advertised for band members at school. Bono (Paul Hewson) on vocals, Adam Clayton on bass guitar and The Edge (Dave Evans) on guitar were part of the original line-up. The band was signed to Island Records in 1980. The same year, they had their first hit single in the UK with *I Will Follow*. The debut album *Boy* failed to chart but it was well received by the music press. It was the release of U2's next albums, *War* (1983) and *The Unforgettable Fire* (1984), that pushed the band

into the international limelight. Early hit singles included *New Year's Day* and *Pride (In the Name of Love)*. U2's appearance at Live Aid in 1985 secured its place in rock history. In 1987, U2's album *The Joshua Tree* was a number one hit in the UK and US. Since then the band has had eight number one albums in the UK and five number one albums in the US. They have also won 22 Grammy Awards and six Brit Awards, including the Outstanding Achievement Award in 2001. U2 is now often referred to as a supergroup. With more than 170 million album sales worldwide they are a tough act to beat.

Scissor Sisters

American band Scissor Sisters was started by lead vocalist Jake Shears and bass guitarist Babydaddy in about 2000. When the pair moved to New York in 2001 Ana Matronic (vocals and percussion), Del Marquis (lead guitar) and Paddy Boom (drums) joined the group. The band say that they have many influences including David Bowie, Chic, the Bee Gees and Duran Duran. Many people make comparisons between their music and that of Elton John. The band scored its first UK top-ten hit single with the cover of the Pink Floyd song *Comfortably Numb,* in 2004. The same year they had top twenty hits with *Take Your Mama*, *Laura*, *Mary* and *Filthy Gorgeous*. The debut album *Scissor Sisters* shot to number one and went on to become the best-selling album of 2004 in the UK. At the 2005 Brit Awards, the band was overwhelmed with emotion when they picked up the awards for International Group, International Breakthrough, and International Album. In 2006, the Scissor Sisters was back with the album *Ta-Dah* which went straight to number one in the UK on the week of its release. With their colourful image and catchy songs, the Scissor Sisters has become one of the biggest selling bands of the past decade.

Index

21st Century Lives

Contents of all books in the series:

WAYLAND